# The Spiritual HEART

## Are You a Sheep, Goat, or Wolf?

As water reflects the face,
so one's Life reflects the Heart.
(Proverbs 27:19 NIV)

# Ron "Too-Tall" Jackson

WESTBOW
PRESS®
A DIVISION OF THOMAS NELSON
& ZONDERVAN

WestBow Press books may be ordered through booksellers or by contacting:

WestBow Press
A Division of Thomas Nelson & Zondervan
1663 Liberty Drive
Bloomington, IN 47403
www.westbowpress.com
1 (866) 928-1240

Because of the dynamic nature of the Internet, any web addresses or links contained in this book may have changed since publication and may no longer be valid. The views expressed in this work are solely those of the author and do not necessarily reflect the views of the publisher, and the publisher hereby disclaims any responsibility for them.

Any people depicted in stock imagery provided by Getty Images are models, and such images are being used for illustrative purposes only. Certain stock imagery © Getty Images.

ISBN: 978-1-6642-0003-6 (sc)
ISBN: 978-1-6642-0004-3 (e)

Library of Congress Control Number: 2020913452

Print information available on the last page.

WestBow Press rev. date: 08/06/2020

Check
Ya
Heart
Ministry
Ronald "Too-tall" Jackson

A sower went out to sow his seed: and as he sowed, some fell by the way side [hard heart]; and it was trodden down, and the fowls of the air devoured it.

And some fell upon a rock [shallow rocky heart]; and as soon as it was sprung up, it withered away, because it lacked moisture.

And some fell among thorns [thorny heart]; and the thorns sprang up with it, and choked it.

And other fell on good ground [good heart], and sprang up, and bare fruit an hundredfold. And when he had said these things, he cried, He that hath ears to hear, let him hear. (Luke 8:5–8 KJV)

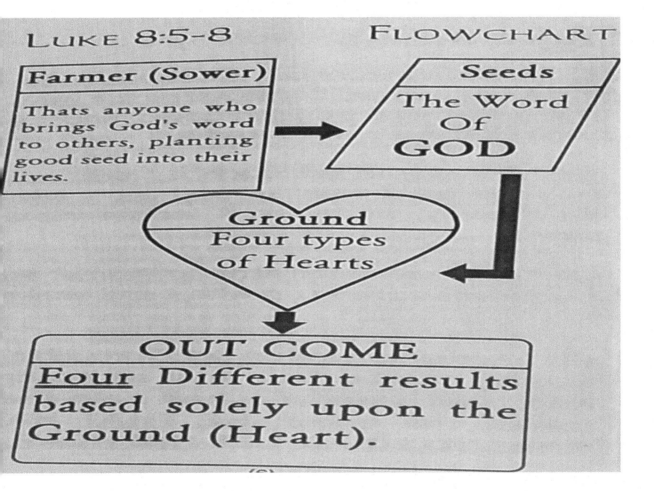

# Ten Spiritual Heart Health Tips
# Revealed during COVID-19

COVID-19: Protect your body. ------------------------------- Tip 1: Guard your mind (belief).

COVID-19: Attacks from the outside-in. -------------------- Tip 2: Spiritual heart attacks come from the outside-in also.

COVI D-19: No vaccine available. ---------------------------- Tip 3: No quick fix; healing takes time.

COVID-19: Avoid large groups. ------------------------------- Tip 4: Avoid yielding to multiple diverse opinions.

COVID-19: Avoid close contact with sick people. -------- Tip 5: Avoid close ties with negative people.

COVID-19: Maintain distancing in public. ------------------ Tip 6: Be careful when making close associations.

COVID-19: Wash your hands. ---------------------------------- Tip 7: Wash and guide your mind with the Word of God.

COVID-19: Wear your mask. ---------------------------------- Tip 8: Watch the words that come out of your mouth.

COVID-19: Avoid touching your face. ----------------------- Tip 9: Protect your thoughts with the Word of God.

COVID-19: Avoid sharing personal items. ------------------ Tip 10: Be careful when sharing your personal information and opinion.

# Introduction

The Heart is hopelessly Dark [Shady] and Deceitful [Dishonest], a puzzle that no one can Figure-Out [Understand].

—Jeremiah 17:9 (MSG)

God has been prompting my spirit to complete this assignment for the past ten years. The COVID-19 pandemic has finally given me the time needed to complete this task. We are in what the Bible calls "the end times," and there is no better time than the present for us to look inside ourselves and see where we actually stand with God.

The biblical word "heart" has been to some degree a mystery in the body of Christ. Did you know that "Jesus" is in the Bible 983 times, "Father" (God) 979 times, and "heart" 830 times? This clearly signifies that the biblical word "heart" is very important to God. Humankind has two types of hearts, a physical heart and a spiritual heart. In the Bible, "heart" refers to our spiritual hearts. The purpose of this book is to gain a better understanding of our spiritual hearts. Our ultimate goal is to demystify the biblical word "heart."

This book also provides comprehensive knowledge by way of my spiritual visual aids and revelation of scripture. As we all know, there is plenty of information on the physical heart but very little information on the spiritual heart. For instance, we know that the physical heart is located inside the chest and pumps blood throughout the body. And we know that exercising and eating right will make the physical heart healthy. But where is the spiritual heart located? What is the purpose of the spiritual heart? What makes the spiritual heart healthy? This book provide answers to these questions and many other inquiries you may have concerning your spiritual heart.

As you read this book, I pray that you not only retain this information but will allow my spiritual visual aids to help you take an objective look at your spiritual heart. My ultimate desire is to inspire you to make the necessary changes so your spiritual heart (ground) will be in a position to transform God's Word (seed) into godly blessings and prosperity in your life. Finally, I give you seven steps to receiving the Holy Spirit.

But I, God, search the Heart and examine the mind. I get to the Heart of the human. I get to the root of things. I treat them as they really are, not as they pretend to be. (Jeremiah 17:10 MEV)

# What Is the Spiritual Heart?

Let us look at the *Strong Concordance* definition of the Greek and Hebrew word "heart."

- ❖ The Greek word for "heart" is "kardia" [kar-dee-ah]—the thoughts or feelings of the mind [2588].
- ❖ The Hebrew word for "heart" is "leb" [labe]—the feelings, the will, and even the intellect; the center of anything; the most interior organ [3820].

# What Is Man?

Man is three dimensional. Man is a spirit, lives inside a body, and has a soul (spiritual heart).

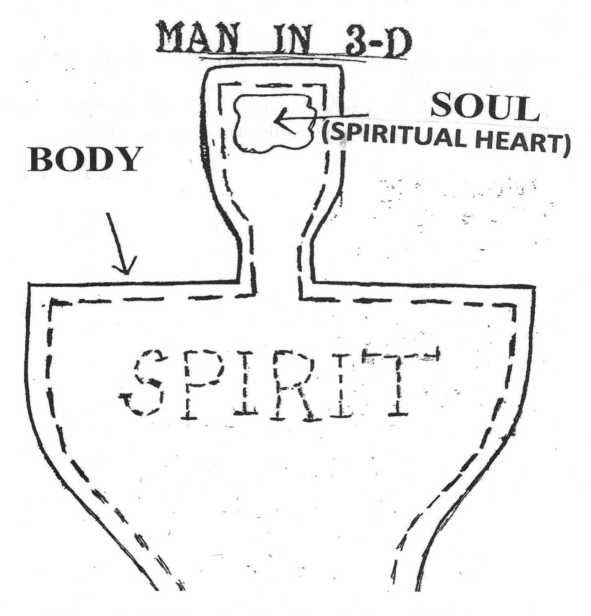

Now may the God of Peace Himself sanctify you [man] completely; and may your whole spirit, soul, and body be preserved blameless at the coming of our Lord Jesus Christ. (1 Thessalonians 5:23 KJV)

Ron "Too-Tall" Jackson

# Where Is the Spiritual Heart Physically Located?

The spiritual heart is the soul (mind, will, emotions). Physically, it is located inside your brain. Though most people touch their chests when referring to the biblical word "heart," the spiritual heart is not in the chest.

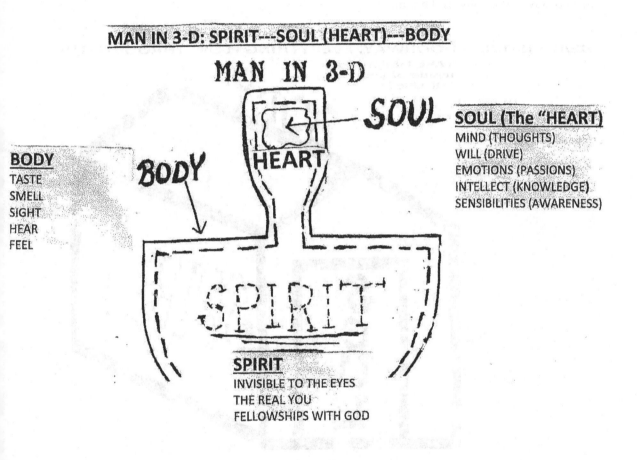

You must love the Lord your God with all your heart and with all your soul, and all your mind. (Matthew 22:37 NLT)

# Where Is the Spiritual Heart Located Spiritually?

The spiritual heart is the soul (mind), which is the doorway to the human spirit. This is where information flows in and out, influencing first your thoughts, then your words, and finally your actions. For example, the outside of the house is the body, the inside of the house is the spirit, and the doorway of the house is the soul.

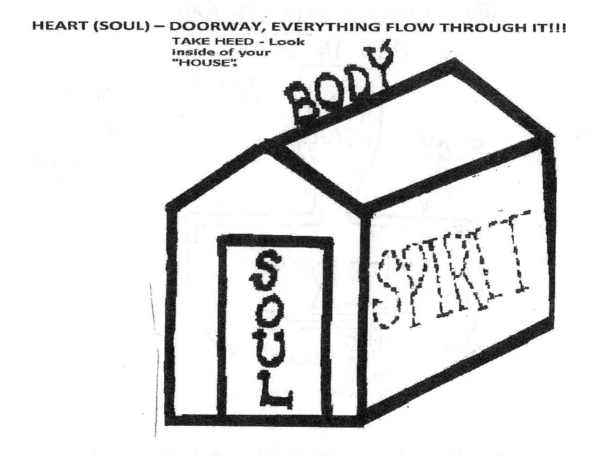

**HEART (SOUL) – DOORWAY, EVERYTHING FLOW THROUGH IT!!!**
**TAKE HEED - Look inside of your "HOUSE":**

BODY

SOUL

SPIRIT

Above all else, guard your heart [soul], for everything flows from it. (Proverbs 4:23 NIV)

Ron "Too-Tall" Jackson

# How Does the Spiritual
# Heart Function?

All of humankind learned information and life experiences flow through the spiritual heart (soul—mind, will, emotions). All thoughts (good and bad) produce godly or worldly actions, resulting in our ultimately obtaining a good, blessed life or a bad, cursed life.

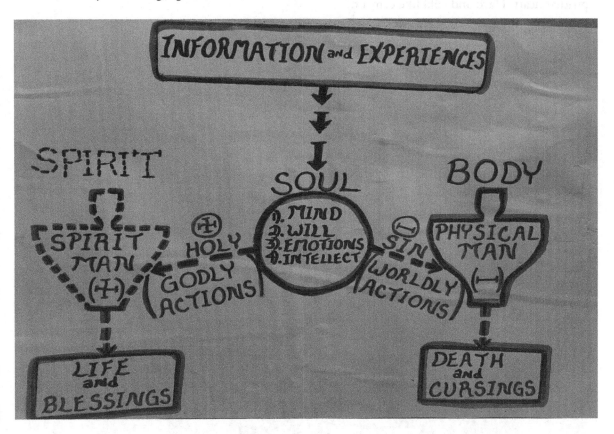

The mind [soul/spiritual heart] governed by the flesh is death, but the mind [soul/spiritual heart] governed by the spirit is life and peace. (Romans 8:6 NIV)

# Spiritual Heart Walking in Darkness—Living Sinfully—Equals Death

This is how your spiritual heart looks when you are living a consistently sinful life. God sees a hard spiritual heart. Hard and cold like cement.

If we say we have an intimate connection with the Father but we continue stumbling around in darkness, then we are lying because we do not live according to truth. (1 John 1:6)

Ron "Too-Tall" Jackson

# Spiritual Heart Walking in the Light—Living Holy—Equals Life

This is how your spiritual heart looks when you are living a consistently holy life. God sees a good spiritual heart. It is moist and rich, like soil.

If we walk step-by-step in the light, where the Father is, then we are ultimately connected to each other through the sacrifice of Jesus His Son. His blood purifies us from all our sins. (1 John 1:7)

# Two Ways We Can See What Is Inside Someone's Spiritual Heart

1.  Listen to the person's words.

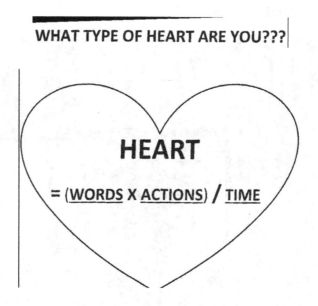

**WHAT TYPE OF HEART ARE YOU???**

**HEART**

**= (WORDS X ACTIONS) / TIME**

Whatever is in your heart determines what you say. (Luke 6:45 NLT)

2.  Watch the person's actions.

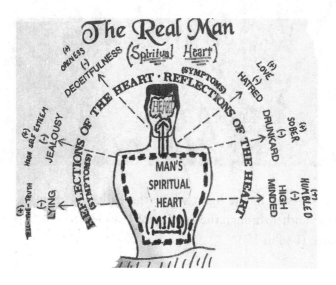

As water reflects the face, so one's life reflects the heart. (Proverbs 27:19 NIV)

# The Four Growth Stages of God's Word inside the Spiritual Heart

God's Word goes through four stages of growth when planted inside the spiritual heart.

1. Seed—hearing and speaking God's Word
2. Plant—accepting and believing God's Word
3. Tree—applying and living by God's Word
4. Fruit—final stage of ultimate maturity; prosperity/success/blessings

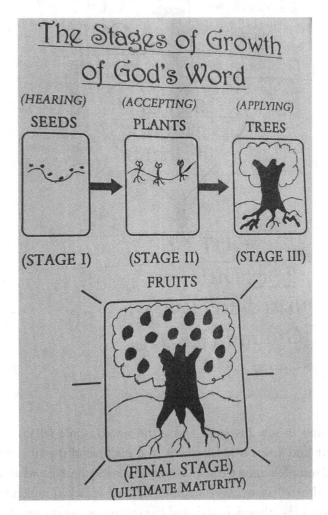

This law scroll must not leave your lips [stage 1] you must memorize it [stage 2] day and night so you can carefully obey [stage 3] all that is written in it. Then you will prosper and be successful [stage 4]. (Joshua 1:8 NET)

The Spiritual Heart

# The Four Types of Spiritual Hearts and Their Four Outcomes

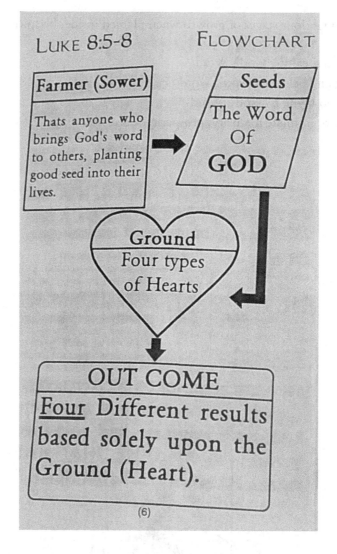

A sower went out to sow his seed: and as he sowed, some fell by the Way Side [1—hard heart]; and it was trodden down, and the fowl of the air devoured it [1—outcome]. And some fell upon a Rock [2—shallow rocky heart]; and as soon as it was sprung up, it withered away [2—outcome], because it lacked moisture. And some fell among Thorns [3—thorny heart]; and the thorns sprang up with it, and choked it [3—outcome]. And other fell on Good Ground [4—good heart], and sprang up, and bare fruit an hundredfold [4—outcome]. And when he had said these things, he cried, He that hath ears to hear, let him hear. (Luke 8:5–8 KJV)

# The First Type of Spiritual Heart: The Hard-Hearted Man

*Planting Seeds in 100 Percent Cement*

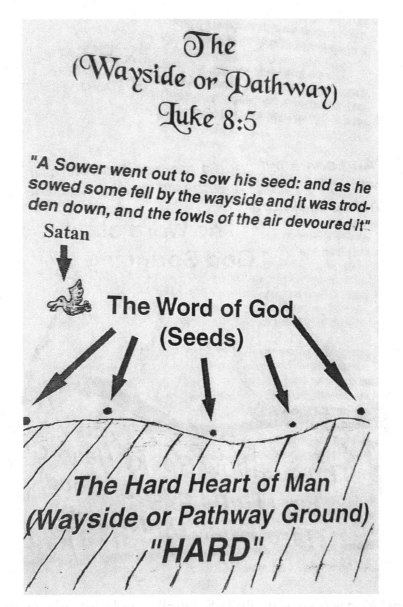

The Seeds [Word of God] that fell on the Footpath [hard-hearted man] represent those who hear the message, only to have the devil come and take it away from their hearts and preventing them from believing and being saved. (Luke 8:12 NLT)

# The Second Type of Spiritual Heart: The Shallow, Rocky-Hearted Man

*Planting Seeds in 5 Percent Good, Rich Soil with 95 Percent Cement Underneath*

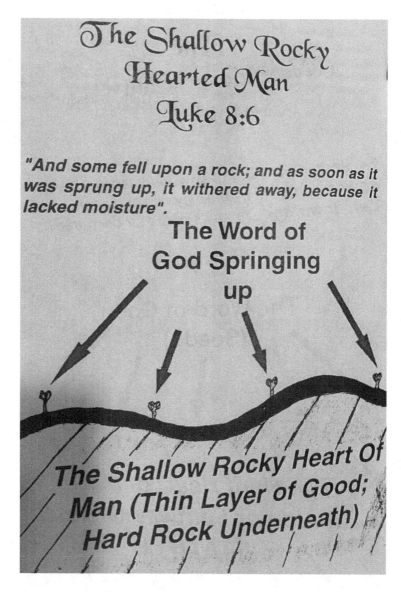

The seeds [Word of God] on the Rocky Soil [shallow, rocky-hearted man] represent those who hear the message and receive it with joy. But since they don't have deep roots, they believe for a while, then they fall away when they face temptation. (Luke 8: 13 NLT)

Ron "Too-Tall" Jackson

# The Third Type of Spiritual Heart: The Thorny-Hearted Man

*Planting Seeds in 100 Percent Good, Rich Soil Full of Thorns*

The Seeds [Word of God] which fell among the Thorns [thorny-hearted man]; these are the ones who have heard, but as they go on their way, they are suffocated with the anxieties and riches and pleasures of this life, and they bring no fruit to maturity. (Luke 8:14 AMP)

# The Fourth Type of Spiritual Heart: The Good-Hearted Man

*Planting Seeds in 100 Percent Good, Rich Soil Free of Cement and Thorns*

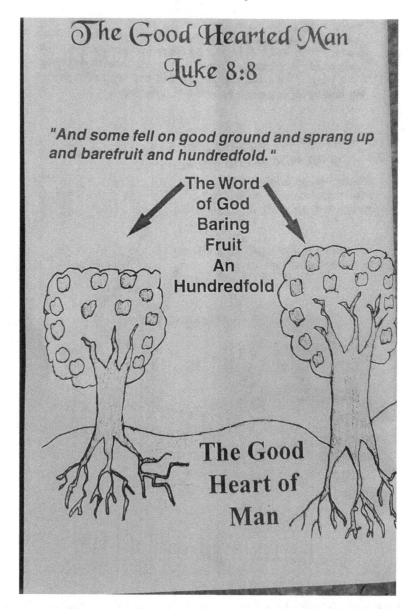

And the Seeds [Word of God] that fell on the Good Soil [good-hearted man] represent honest, good-hearted people who hear God's word, cling to it, and patiently produce a huge harvest. (Luke 8:15 NLT)

# The Spiritual Heart before Salvation: Born a Sinner

Adam's sin separated man from God. Therefore, all men are born into this world a sinner—unrighteous—and when man dies physically, he will have eternal death—hell.

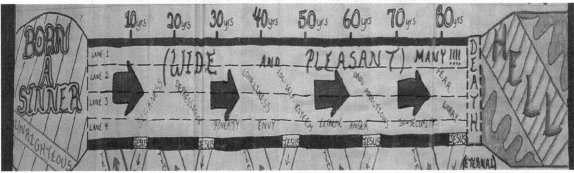

When Adam sinned, sin entered the world, Adam's sin brought death, so death spread to everyone, for everyone sinned. (Romans 5:12 NLT)

# The Spiritual Heart after Salvation: Jesus Saves

God sent his Son, Jesus, to die on the cross to establish a relationship with man so whoever believes in Jesus Christ will have eternal life in heaven.

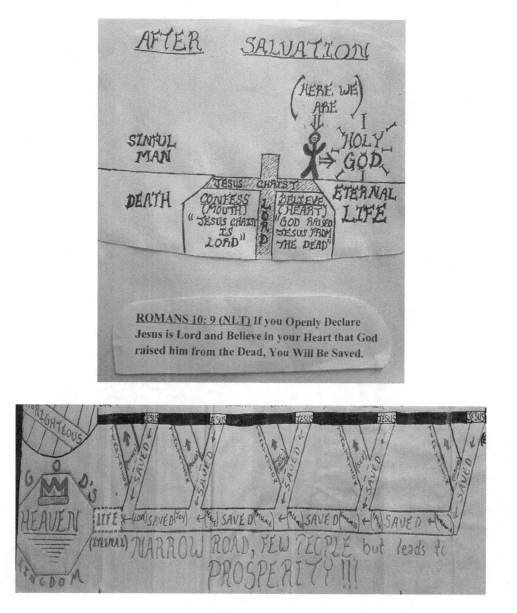

If you openly declare that Jesus is Lord and believe in your heart that God raised him from the dead, you will be saved. (Romans 10:9 NLT)

# First: Hard-Hearted Man Rejected Jesus (Nonbeliever)

Seeds—God's Word—never enter the hard ground, the heart. Satan takes seeds—God's Word—from the ground, resulting in no growth of God's Word inside the heart.

*Outcome:* Hard-hearted man rejected the Word of God, Jesus (nonbeliever).

## The (Wayside or Pathway) Luke 8:5

"A Sower went out to sow his seed: and as he sowed some fell by the wayside and it was trodden down, and the fowls of the air devoured it"

Satan

**The Word of God (Seeds)**

**The Hard Heart of Man (Wayside or Pathway Ground) "HARD"**

The seeds that fell on the footpath [hard-hearted man] represent those who hear the message, only to have the devil come and take it away from their hearts and prevent them from believing and being saved. (Luke 8:12 NLT)

Ron "Too-Tall" Jackson

# First: Hard-Hearted Man,
# Dull Spiritual Perceiver

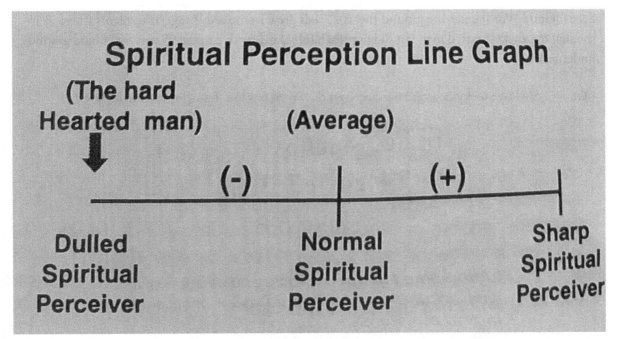

The hard-hearted man classifies as a dull spiritual perceiver due to hardness (100 percent) inside the heart. Characteristics of a hard-hearted person are being stubborn, a refusal to believe, a lack of faith, being stiff-necked, and spiritual blindness.

# Second: Shallow, Rocky-Hearted Man Received Jesus, Immature Believer

Seeds [God's Word] enter the ground (heart). Seeds grew from seeds (stage 1) to plants (stage 2) in the shallow, rocky-hearted man but did not reach full maturity due to the 95 percent of hard ground underneath.

*Outcome:* Shallow, rocky-hearted man received the Word of God, Jesus (immature believer).

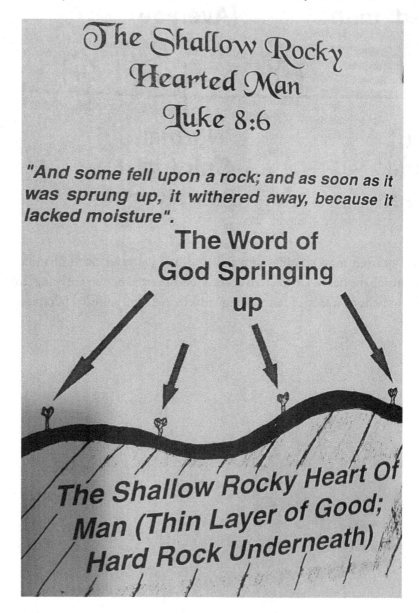

Ron "Too-Tall" Jackson

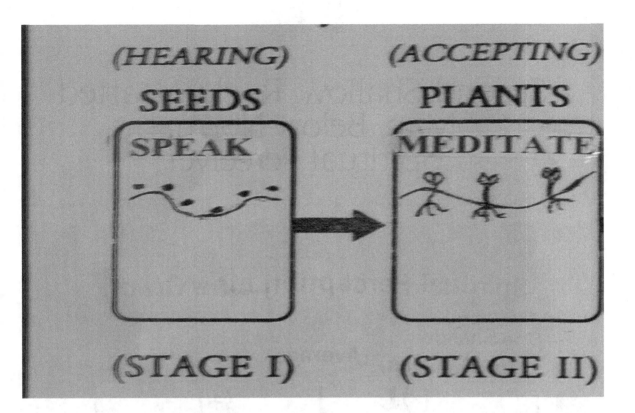

The seeds on the rocky soil represent those who hear the message and receive it with joy. But since they don't have deep roots, they believe for a while, then they fall away when they face temptation. (Luke 8:13 NLT)

# Second: Shallow, Rocky-Hearted Man, Below-Normal Spiritual Perceiver

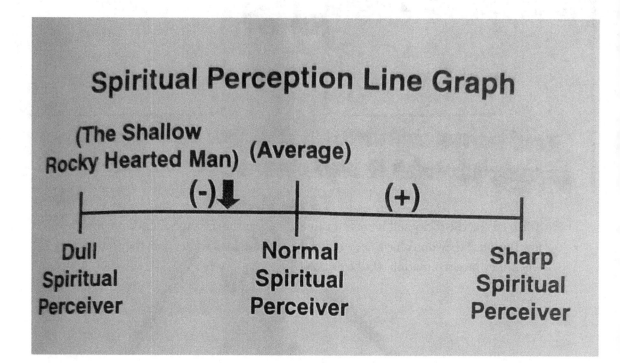

The shallow, rocky-hearted man classifies as a below-normal spiritual perceiver due to the 95 percent of hardness inside the heart. Anytime hardness exists inside the heart, spiritual perception will be limited. The amount of hardness inside the heart directly affects the length of time the heart is able to hold the Word of God. The greater the hardness, the shorter the preservation period, the time the Word of God is able to live inside the heart.

# Third: Thorny-Hearted Man Received Jesus, Immature Believer

Seeds (God's Word) enter the ground (heart). Seeds grew from seeds (stage 1) to plants (stage 2) in the thorny-hearted man but did not reach full maturity due to the thorns—the cares, riches, and pleasures of this life.

*Outcome:* The thorny-hearted man received the Word of God, Jesus (immature believer).

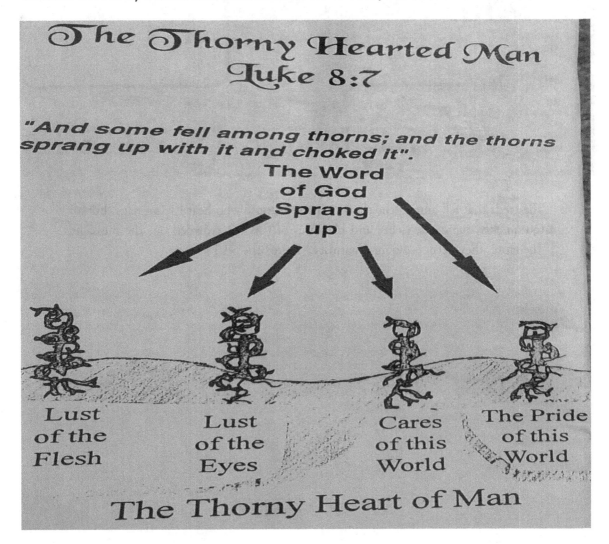

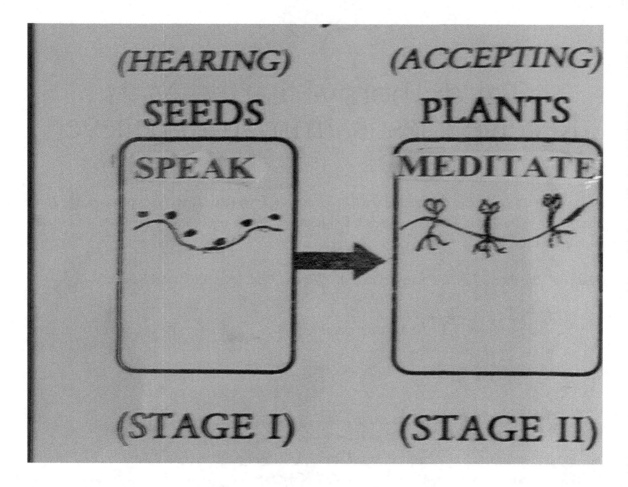

The seeds that fell among the thorns represent those who hear the message, but all too quickly, the cares, riches and pleasures of this life crowded out the message. Therefore, they never grow into maturity. (Luke 8:14 NLT)

# Third: Thorny-Hearted Man, Above-Normal Spiritual Perceiver

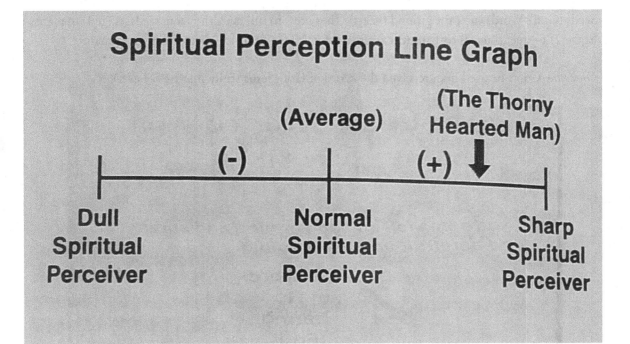

The thorny-hearted man classifies as an above-normal spiritual perceiver because there is no hardness inside the heart. Hardness limits you from understanding and believing the Word of God. If Satan cannot cause hardness, he will try to plant thorns (temptations) inside the heart because Satan knows if this heart is left alone, it will produce fruit. The thorny-hearted man yielded to Satan's thorns—lust of the eyes and flesh, cares of this world, and the pride of life.

# Fourth: Good-Hearted Man Received Jesus, Fully Mature Believer

Seeds (God's Word) enter the ground (heart). They grew to full maturity from seeds (stage 1) to plants (stage 2) to tree (stage 3) to-fruit (the ultimate, final stage 4) inside the good-hearted man.

*Outcome:* Good-hearted man received the Word of God, Jesus (fully mature believer).

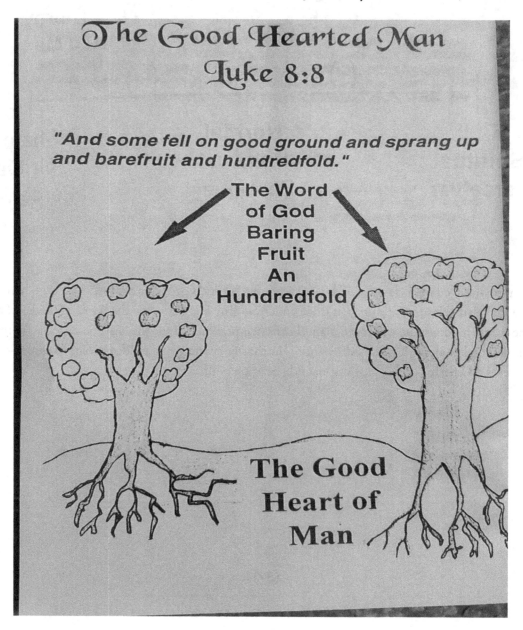

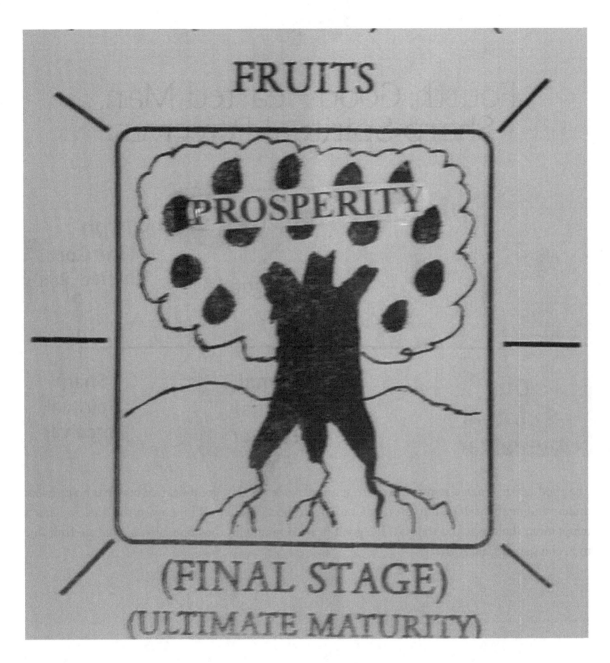

And the seeds that fell on the good soil represent honest, good-hearted people who hear God's word, cling to it, and patiently produce a huge harvest. (Luke 8:15 NLT)

# Fourth: Good-Hearted Man, Sharp Spiritual Perceiver

## Spiritual Perception Line Graph

(The Good Hearted Man)

(Average)

(-)        (+)

Dull Spiritual Perceiver

Normal Spiritual Perceiver

Sharp Spiritual Perceiver

The good-hearted man classifies as a sharp spiritual perceiver. The good-hearted man has no problem understanding, believing, and obeying God's Word because they will not open the door to Satan's temptations (hardness and thorns). The good-hearted man will, therefore, always produce fruit due to his honest and sincere heart.

# The Good-Hearted Man Produces the Fruit of the Spirit

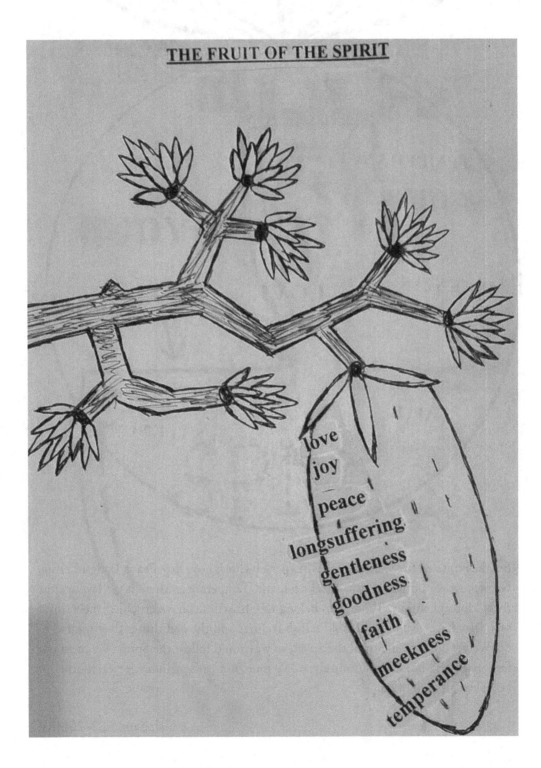

THE FRUIT OF THE SPIRIT

love
joy
peace
longsuffering
gentleness
goodness
faith
meekness
temperance

# THE FRUIT OF THE SPIRIT

But the Fruit that the Spirit produces in a person's life is Love, Joy, Peace, Longsuffering, Gentleness, Goodness, Faith, Meekness, and Temperance. There is no law against these kinds of things. Those who belong to Christ Jesus have crucified their sinful self. They have given up their old selfish feelings and the evil things they wanted to do. We get our new life from the Spirit, so we should follow the Spirit. We must not feel proud and boast about ourselves. We must not cause trouble for each other or be jealous of each other.

Galatians 5:22–26 ERV

Ron "Too-Tall" Jackson

# The Four Spiritual Hearts and Their Relationship to Salvation

This is where the four spiritual hearts are located on the road to salvation.

1. - Hard-hearted man (see wide road): Rejected Jesus—nonbeliever
2. - Shallow, rocky-hearted man (see Jesus road): Received Jesus but yields to temptation—immature believer
3. - Thorny-hearted man (see Jesus road): Received Jesus but yields to temptation—immature believer
4. - Good-hearted man (see narrow road): Received Jesus, resisted temptation—fully mature believer

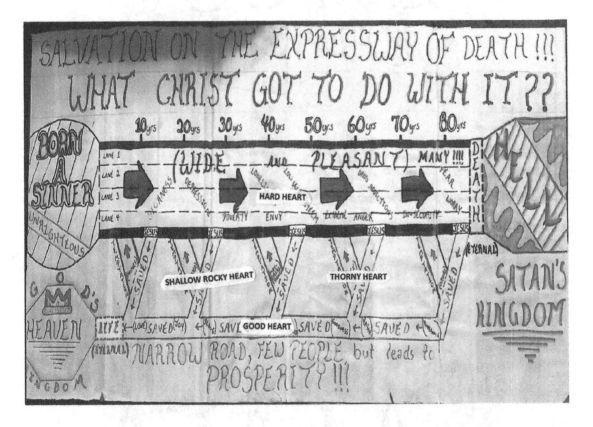

Heaven can be entered only through the Narrow Gate the highway to Hell is Broad, and its gate is Wide enough for All The Multitudes who choose its Easy Way. But the gateway to Life is Small, and the road is Narrow, and only a Few ever find it. (Matthew 7:13–14 TLB)

# The Imaginary/Perfect Church:

**Overseer (Pastor)—Feed (Teach)—Flock (100 Percent Sheep)**

The imaginary/perfect church is a congregation full of humbled/submitted-sheep led by the pastor (overseer).

The Sheep listen to the voice of the Shepherd. He calls his own sheep by name and leads them out. When the Shepherd walks ahead of them, they follow him because they know his voice. (John 10:3–5 NLV)

# The Real/Imperfect Church:

## Overseer (Pastor)—Feed (Teach)—Flock (Sheep, Goats, Wolves)

The real/imperfect church is a congregation with sheep, goats, and wolves. Greedy wolves upfront fight for leadership. Rebellious goats cause distraction by separating humble sheep, trying to prevent them from reaching their ultimate goal of full maturity and prosperity that God intended.

All nations will be gathered before Him, and He will separate them one from another, as a Shepherd divides his Sheep from the Goats. And he will set the Sheep on his right hand, but the Goats on the left. (Matthew 25:32–33 NKJV)

For I know this, that after my departure savage Wolves will come in among you, not sparing the Flock. (Acts 20:2 NKJV)

# First Type of Believer (Church Member)—Goat (Shallow, Rocky-Hearted Man)

Goat—Greek word *eriphion* (er-if'-ee-on)

Definition: kidling (immature), not submissive to Christ, rebellious against God.

Goats are church members who never reach their full maturity due to their rebellious hearts (shallow rocky hearts, that prevented God's Word from growing and reaching full maturity.

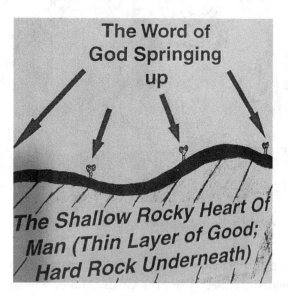

He will put … the Goats on his Left. Then he will say to those on his Left, "Depart from me, you who are cursed, into the eternal fire prepared for the devil and his angels. (Matthew 25:33, 41 NIV)

# Do You Have the Spiritual Heart of a Goat?

The seven characteristics of a goat (shallow, rocky-hearted man):

1. Goats are difficult to lead.
2. Goats are the majority of church membership.
3. Goats love sowing discord and division.
4. Goats hinder the progress of God's Word by distracting sheep.
5. Goats are comfortable in chaotic church environments; goats hate peace.
6. Goats cause dissension and confusion by creating an undercurrent of negative gossip.
7. Goats are unfaithful members who are short-sermon lovers, clock-watchers, mind drifters, non-note takers, Bible forgetters, and non-tithers.

# Second Type of Believer (Church Member)—Wolf (Thorny-Hearted Man)

Wolf—Greek word *lukos* (loo'-kos)

Definition: A wolf eats flesh, hunts in packs, and teams up on prey.

<u>Wolves</u> are church members who yield to temptations—lust of the flesh, lust of the eyes, cares of this world, and the pride of life—choking out God's Word due to their thorny hearts that fuel wolves' desires to attack sheep.

The Thorny Heart of Man

Watch out for false prophets. They come to you in Sheep's Clothing, but inwardly they are Ferocious Wolves. (Matthew 7:15 NIV)

Ron "Too-Tall" Jackson

# Do You Have the Spiritual Heart of a Wolf?

The seven characteristics of a wolf (thorny-hearted man):

1.  Wolves are close to impossible to lead successfully.
2.  Wolves are very flexible; they can operate in chaotic or peaceful church environments.
3.  Wolves love to attack sheep [anointed mature believers] as sheep are Wolves' biggest threat (enemies).
4.  Wolves love to be in control; they desire church leadership positions, so they can set their eyes on their prey (sheep).
5.  Wolves deceive most church members and those in church leadership by presenting themselves outwardly as sheep.
6.  Wolves are great actors/imitators/hypocrites/phonies.
7.  Wolves seek to be the pastor's top leaders by doing anything to obtain church leadership.

# Third Type of Believer (Church Member)—Sheep (Good-Hearted Man), God's Best

Sheep—Greek word *probaton* (prob'-at-on)

Definition: Something that walks forward (progresses slowly), advances, goes farther.

<u>Sheep</u> are believers who reached full maturity due to their good hearts. Sheep allowed the Word of God to grow from seed-to-plant-to-tree-to-fruit.

He will put the Sheep on his Right … Then the King will say to those on his Right, "Come, you who are blessed by my Father; take your inheritance, the kingdom has prepared … (Matthew 25:33–34 NIV)

# Do You Have the Spiritual Heart of a Sheep?

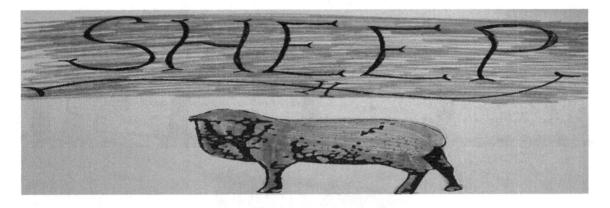

The seven characteristics of a sheep (good-hearted man), God's best:

1. Sheep are a pleasure to lead. They submit to authority and mind their own business.
2. Sheep are loyal and devoted church members.
3. Sheep are the elite minority in church membership.
4. Sheep love peaceful and loving church environments; sheep often leave unpeaceful church environments.
5. Sheep attend church for the Word of God; they are present with Bibles, pens, and pads to receive God's Word.
6. Sheep are generous in their giving of tithes and offerings.
7. Sheep are often attacked by the wolves through deception and by goats through agitation.

# Which Spiritual Heart Are You—Sheep, Goat, or Wolf?

WHICH SPIRITUAL HEART ARE YOU???

HARD GOAT (ROCKY) WOLF (THORNY) SHEEP (GOOD)

Ron "Too-Tall" Jackson

# Self-Assessment

Above all else, Guard Your Heart, for it is the Well Spring [Issues] of Life.

Proverbs 4:23 NIV

- Hard-Hearted Man (Nonbeliever): Have you ever rejected the plan of salvation? Does the Word of God go in one ear and out the other? Do you say the Word of God does not apply to you? Do you believe the Bible is not true? Do you avoid attending church?

  - ❑ If you answered yes to these questions, you probably have a hard spiritual heart and are a nonbeliever.

- Shallow, Rocky-Hearted Man (Immature Believer—"Goat"): Have you received Jesus as your Lord and Savior? Do you find yourself going against church rules a lot? Do you participate in negative gossip with church members? Do you like it when church members disagree with each other?

  - ❑ If you answered yes to these questions, you probably have a shallow, rocky spiritual heart and are a goat.

- Thorny-Hearted Man (Immature Believer—"Wolf"): Have you received Jesus as your Lord and Savior? Do you find ways to get back at church members through lying, gossiping, plotting, and so on? Do you seek to obtain top leadership positions in the church at any cost, even backstabbing, lying, and so on? Are you one way outwardly but inwardly you really are someone else? Do you find yourself teaming up with others to attack a particular church member (a "sheep") you do not like?

  - ❑ If you answered yes to these questions, you probably have a thorny spiritual heart and are a wolf.

- Good-Hearted Man (Fully Mature Believer—"Sheep"): Have you received Jesus as your Lord and Savior? Do you love hearing the Word of God? Do you try to live by the Word of God? Do you love being in a peaceful church environment? Are you a faithful tither and offering giver? Are you often attacked by other church members? Has God blessed you tremendously over the years in marriage, financially, emotionally, spiritually, and so on?

  - ❑ If you answered yes to these questions, you probably have a good spiritual heart and are a sheep.

Please, please, please take an objective look, and see what is taking place inside your spiritual heart. My ultimate desire is to inspire you to make the necessary changes so your spiritual heart (ground) will be in a position to transform God's Word (seed) into godly blessings and prosperity in your life.

But I, God, search the Heart and examine the mind. I get to the Heart of the human. I get to the root of things. I treat them as they really are, not as they pretend to be. (Jeremiah 17:10 MEV)

Ron "Too-Tall" Jackson

# The Seven Steps in Receiving God's Power, the Holy Spirit

Now that you have evaluated your spiritual heart, it is time to be filled with the Holy Spirit and power—ability, efficiency, and might. Here are the seven steps necessary to receive the Holy Spirit. I pray that God will fill you with his Spirit, enduing you with his power in Jesus's name.

But you shall receive Power [Ability, Efficiency, and Might] when the Holy Spirit has come upon you … (Acts 1:8 AMPC)

# The First Step to Receiving the Holy Spirit

The Holy Spirit has been given to us since the Day of Pentecost, fifty days after Passover. It is up to you to receive the Holy Spirit.

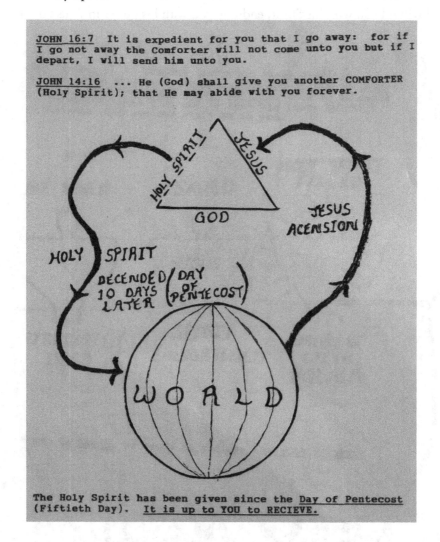

But I tell you that I am going to do what is best for you. That is why I am going away. The Holy Spirit cannot come to help you until I leave. But after I am gone, I will send the Spirit to you. (John 16:7 CEV)

Then I will ask the Father to send you the Holy Spirit who will help you and always be with you. (John 14:16 CEV)

Ron "Too-Tall" Jackson

# The Second Step to Receiving the Holy Spirit

Anyone who is saved—a believer who received Jesus—is eligible to receive the Holy Spirit.

… the Holy Spirit who will help you and always be with you. The Spirit will show you what is true. The people of this world cannot accept the Spirit, because they do not see or know him. But you know the Spirit, who is with you and will keep on living in you. (John 14:16–17 CEV)

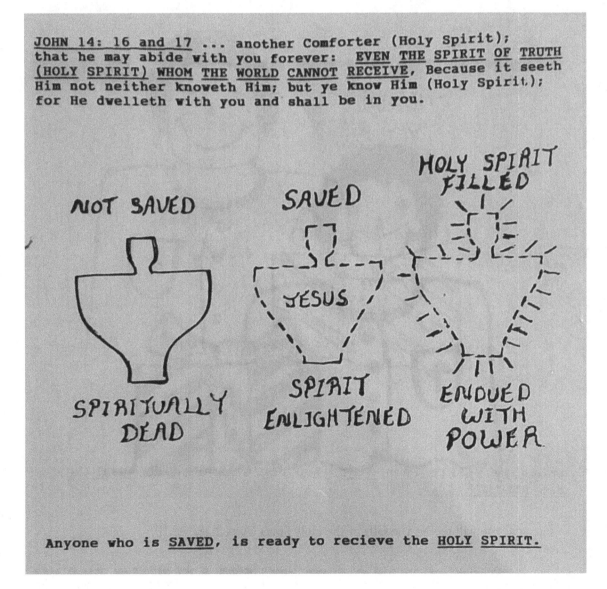

JOHN 14: 16 and 17 ... another Comforter (Holy Spirit); that he may abide with you forever: EVEN THE SPIRIT OF TRUTH (HOLY SPIRIT) WHOM THE WORLD CANNOT RECEIVE, Because it seeth Him not neither knoweth Him; but ye know Him (Holy Spirit); for He dwelleth with you and shall be in you.

NOT SAVED

SAVED

HOLY SPIRIT FILLED

JESUS

SPIRITUALLY DEAD

SPIRIT ENLIGHTENED

ENDUED WITH POWER

Anyone who is SAVED, is ready to recieve the HOLY SPIRIT.

# The Third Step to Receiving the Holy Spirit

The Holy Spirit is a gift. You don't have to do anything but receive it.

ACTS 2: 38c ... And ye shall recieve the GIFT, of the HOLY SPIRIT (Ghost).

THANK YOU!!!

HOLY SPIRIT

HOLY SPIRIT

The Holy Spirit is a GIFT, You don't have to do ANYTHING but RECIEVE IT.

... and you will receive the Gift of the Holy Spirit (Acts 2:38c AMP)

Ron "Too-Tall" Jackson

# The Fourth Step to Receiving the Holy Spirit

Expect to receive the Holy Spirit when hands are laid on you. However, you can also receive the Holy Spirit when you are alone by lifting your hands and praying unto God.

ACTS 8: 17 Then LAID THEY THEIR HANDS ON THEM and they recieved the HOLY GHOST. (Peter and John laid hands on the Samaritan Believers.)

Expect to recieve the HOLY SPIRIT when HANDS ARE LAID ON YOU.

Then Peter and John laid their hands on them [one by one], and they received the Holy Spirit. (Acts 8:17 AMP)

# The Fifth Step to Receiving the Holy Spirit

After your initial experience, you will be able to speak and pray in an unknown tongue at will.

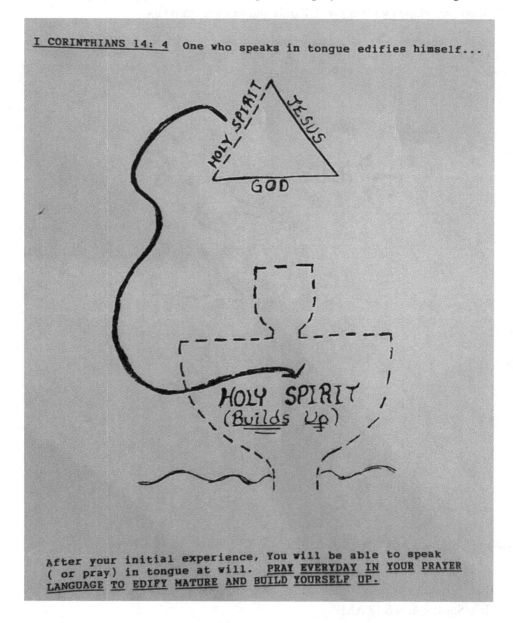

Pray every day in your prayer language to edify—mature and build—yourself up.

One who speaks in a tongue edifies himself. (1 Corinthians 14:4 AMP)

Ron "Too-Tall" Jackson

# The Sixth Step to Receiving the Holy Spirit

You will not understand what you are saying.

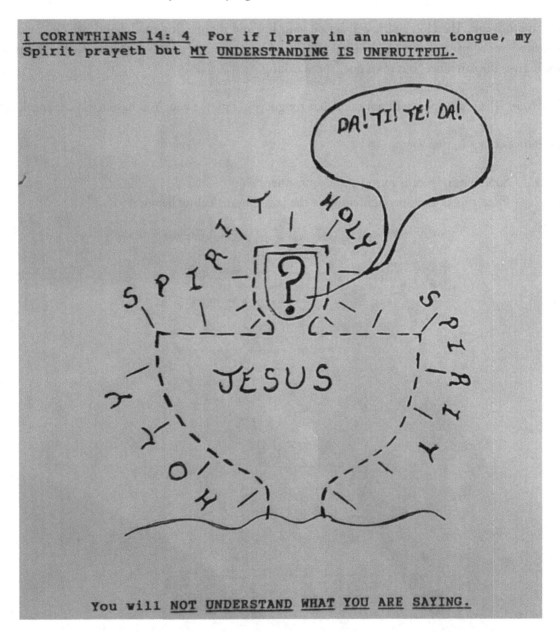

For if I pray in a language I don't understand, my spirit is praying, but I don't know what I am saying. (1 Corinthians 14:14 TLB)

# The Seventh Step to Receiving the Holy Spirit

Now lift your hands, pray, and ask God to fill you with his Spirit. Start speaking in tongues!

You are to speak. The Holy Spirit will act on your lips and tongue (internally) and put supernatural words on your lips. But you need to put the sound to action and speak out (externally). The Holy Spirit gives the utterance, but man does the speaking.

*Important:* The Holy Spirit will not take your tongue and talk for you. You have to do the speaking.

Utterance comes in two ways:

1. - Supernatural words form inside your inner being.
2. - Fluttering of the lips, tightening of the jaw, tongue feeling heavy.

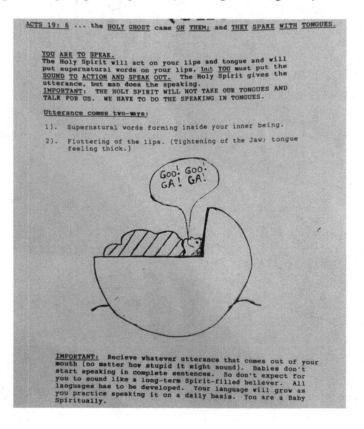

... the Holy Spirit came on them, and They Began Speaking in unknown tongues [languages]. (Acts19:6 AMP)

Ron "Too-Tall" Jackson

# Conclusion

**The Spiritual Heart Is the <u>Real Man, t</u>he Real You**

Out of all the things Jesus could have used to symbolize the heart of man, Jesus used the ground. I feel like Jesus used the ground because it is something that we use the most but pay the least attention to. We have a tendency to take the ground for granted. People in general make mistakes on land decisions more than anything. Land can look one way on the outside that is very different on the Inside. People are the same way.

Have you ever met someone who seemed to be very nice at first, but as time passed, you found out he or she was doing things against you behind your back, and you noticed a difference in their attitude toward you? Even when the person is in your presence, he or she will still try to pretend as if nothing is going on. You are now beginning to see the "real man," not the "superficial man" presented to you at the beginning of the relationship. No matter how much anyone tries to camouflage what is going on inside his or her spiritual heart, pretending to be something the person is not, the real man will eventually manifest over time. No one but God, the Creator, can see the entire spiritual heart of man. However, if you pay careful attention to a person's actions, you will see enough of his or her spiritual heart to know where that person stands. The Bible confirms this by saying, "by their fruit (actions), you will know them" (Matthew 7:16).

Before any of our actions manifest outwardly, they have to start inwardly, in our spiritual hearts. Our inner lives control our outward lives. This is why Jesus put a strong emphasis on our spiritual hearts. Jesus is telling us that we should work from the inside-out, not outside-in. God isn't concerned about how much money we have in the bank, what high position we have in our jobs or in the church, our big houses and nice cars, or how many influential people we have as friends. God is only concerned about our spiritual hearts.

I pray that this book will allow you to take an objective look at your spiritual heart because if you take care of it, everything in your life will take care of itself. Finally, if you did not receive the Holy Spirit the first time you went through the seven steps, don't give up. Keep trying until you receive it and God's power. It takes a couple of times for some people. May God bless you in your godly walk with him.

Above all else, Guard your Heart [spiritual heart], for everything flows from it. (Proverbs 4:23 NIV)

# About the Author

Ron "Too-Tall" Jackson currently lives in Memphis, Tennessee; happily married with his lovely sweet wife Debra Williams-Jackson. He is the founder of the Check-Ya-Heart "Real Prosperity" Ministry, whose purpose is to help others reach full prosperity from the heart. By checking your heart and finding out what is stopping the Word of God from growing there, you can obtain the blessings that God has created for you to possess and enjoy life through the Word of God.

Printed in the United States
By Bookmasters